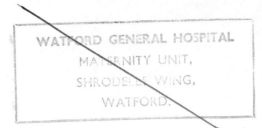

Clinics in Developmental Medicine No. 30

Developmental Screening
0-5 Years

D F Egan

R S Illingworth

R C Mac Keith

LONDON:

Spastics International Medical Publications

in Association with

William Heinemann Medical Books Ltd

Contents

SBN 433-16501-4

© 1969 Spastics International Medical Publications

Reprinted 1971

Printed in England at THE LAVENHAM PRESS LTD., Lavenham, Suffolk.

Introduction

Two aspects of paediatrics will, from now onwards, play increasingly large parts: the promotion of health — physical, mental and social — and the care of children with chronic handicaps. For both these reasons there is in all countries an increasing interest in the developmental aspects of paediatrics.

Children with chronic handicaps, whether of heart and lungs, metabolism or of cerebral origin usually have multiple rather than single handicaps. For example, the child with congenital heart disease is more than usually liable to have visual disorders. These chronic handicaps are often present from early life, and secondary complications — medical, educational and social — frequently occur. They can be prevented only if comprehensive management of the problems of the child and his family are started early enough; early identification is therefore essential.

Handicaps, and especially those of cerebral origin, lead to delay in development. If this delay is recognised, it becomes possible by further examination to identify the underlying handicap or handicaps. The child with developmental delay can be identified by developmental examinations. If the children with handicaps are to be identified early, then *all* infants and children must have a series of periodic developmental screening examinations. The screening is not a once-for-all procedure; as he grows older the child is examined to see if the appropriate new skills have emerged. These developmental screening examinations need not be time-consuming and they should be part of any medical examination of a child — well or ill — just as much as listening to the child's heart.

In this aspect of his work the responsibility of the doctor who sees any child is three-fold. It is to help the child to develop his full potential, to suspect or detect any delay in development and to ensure that every child for whom he is responsible receives periodic developmental screening. If he finds reason to suspect that the child has, in any way, delayed development, he refers him to an expert for further assessment and treatment and for guidance of the parents. The developmental screening techniques described in this book are no substitute for expert detailed and lengthy comprehensive assessment of the defects causing the developmental delay, but they are the essential basis for early assessment, diagnosis and treatment.

In planning the developmental screening examinations it is useful to consider the child's function in four main areas, namely, locomotion and posture; vision and fine manipulation; hearing, language and speech; and everyday skills and social development (including emotional relationships). The screening examinations are most conveniently carried out at certain key ages, for example, 6 weeks, 6 months, 10 months, 18 months, 2 years, 3 years and 4½ years. The descriptions which follow in this book are arranged accordingly.

In many countries most children are seen several times in their first year for advice, routine examination, and immunisation by their family doctor or paediatri-

cian or by the medical officer at their child welfare ('well baby') clinic. The value —
and the interest — of such periodic visits will be considerably enhanced by competent
developmental screening examinations.

The content of this book derives from the experience of the members of the
working party with children of all ages. Beyond this there are two main sources of
information: firstly the work of physicians, including pioneers such as Arnold
Gesell and Albrecht Peiper, and present-day workers, of whom two members of the
working party, Mary Sheridan and Ronald Illingworth, may be mentioned; secondly
the work of psychologists, such as Nancy Bayley and Ruth Griffiths, who have
designed and applied standardized testing procedures for use with young children.
Sometimes the paediatrician has felt that the psychologist's methods neglect observation of the quality of the child's response and that with very young children numerical
quotients are liable to misuse, while the psychologist has felt that the paediatrician's
observations lack standardisation. But work in this field goes on and with collabora-
tion will be even more fruitful. There is, however, an urgent need for a manual for
busy doctors to use in their clinics, and drawing on collective knowledge, the
working party described below has provided what seems to us as accurate an account
of the child's functioning at different ages as is possible at the moment and one
which is full enough, but not too full, to serve the doctor dealing with children. We
have included some references in the text and we give a few key texts in a bibliography
and the reader who wishes to know more will have no difficulty if he consults
colleagues of his own and other disciplines and visits his library.

With Dorothy Egan as Chairman, a working party of experts from paediatrics,
public health, education, psychology and psychiatry, sponsored by the Medical
Education and Information Unit of the Spastics Society, has met over a period of 18
months to produce a schedule of the minimum developmental examinations whereby
reliable screening can, with practice, be carried out quickly*. This is described in this
book. The working party is grateful to Ronald Illingworth who prepared the first
draft of the book.

The working party hope that this book will be found useful to paediatricians,
family doctors and to doctors working in children's preventive services, many of
whom have already shown exemplary interest in this aspect of medical care. With a
background of many years of experience, we in the U.K. can make a special contribu-
tion in this field of preventive paediatrics. We feel that any country that wishes to
raise the quality of its child care will do well to ensure competent periodic developmental paediatric screening examinations of all infants and young children. The
proportion of children with major defects detected under the age of 12 months and of
other defects detected before the child is of school age provide good criteria of the
quality of paediatric services.

*Members of the Working Party were:

Martin C. O. Bax	John Hutt	Roger Robinson
(Secretary 1968-69)	Ronald S. Illingworth	(Secretary 1966)
Dorothy F. Egan (Chairman)	Ronald C. Mac Keith	Michael Rutter
Jessie Francis-Williams	Thomas E. Oppé	Mary D. Sheridan
Ronald Gold	Barry Pless	Jack Tizard
Kenneth S. Holt	Grace Rawlings	John Wilson
(Secretary 1967-8)		

Aim

This book is intended to be a guide to rapid successive screening developmental examinations in busy child welfare or well baby clinics, doctors' surgeries or offices and out-patient departments of Children's Units. It is hoped that it will help the busy doctor to satisfy himself that the child is developing normally and to recognise when there is doubt about this so that expert advice can be sought. It is also hoped that it will provide a means to a useful record of the development of individual children. It is in no way intended, however, to provide a comprehensive discourse on the development or developmental examination of the child.

The Examination of the Child

The routine medical examination of any baby, in any clinic, surgery, office, home or hospital, must include the following:

A general physical examination
A developmental screening examination

    (a) gross motor function
    (b) vision and fine manipulation
    (c) hearing and language
    (d) skills and social reactions.

General Physical Examination

The general physical examination will include an assessment of the child's nutrition, of his general health and responsiveness to his environment. The examiner will also evaluate the level of the mother's physical care and note her attitude to her baby, and the affection which she shows to him.

The full clinical examination is not described here in detail but certain items which relate particularly to the developmental examination will be discussed. The clinical examination will include the following items:

Weight (and evaluation of the deviation of this from the mean for age, making allowance where necessary for short gestation and for low birth weight).

Measurement of the maximum head circumference (and evaluating this in relation to the age *and weight* of the baby).

Inspection of the eyes for cataract etc. (Vision is tested as part of developmental screening).

Inspection of ears to exclude purulent discharge and, when indicated, examination with an electric auriscope. (Hearing is tested in the developmental screening).

1

Examination of heart, lungs, abdomen. (Auscultation of the heart and examination of the femoral pulses can only be done if the infant is not crying; a comforter 'dummy' may be useful.)

Evaluation of muscle tone and tendon reflexes.

Examination of hips for dislocation or subluxation.

Examination of the genitalia.

Examination of the skin.

Inspection of the sacral region (in the midline) of the back for congenital dermal sinus.

Test for phenylpyruvic acid in urine (after the age of 5 weeks) or, preferably, blood test for the serum phenylalanine level (after the age of 6 days).

Head Circumference

The maximum head circumference must be measured in all babies. It is an essential part of the routine examination

The tape measure is passed round his forehead above the eyes, and round the occiput at a rather lower level to give the maximum head circumference. The measurement is made twice. Care must be taken to ensure that the tape measure has not stretched, and thereby become inaccurate. A metal tape is preferable although it is more difficult to manage than a plastic or woven one.

The head measurement is necessary because the size of the skull reflects the growth and size of the cranial contents. If the brain does not grow properly, as in mental subnormality, the head circumference is usually small. Measurement of the head circumference is also essential for the early detection of hydrocephalus.

The head circumference at birth in normal full term infants is usually $13\frac{3}{4}$ inches (35 cms.). The rate of gain of head circumference in early months is $\frac{1}{2}$ inch per month for the first 5 months and then slows to $\frac{1}{4}$ inch a month for the rest of the first year; from which the expected mean circumference for any age under 1 year can be calculated. The charts (Fig. 1a and b) give the average head size at various ages together with the limits of common variation of normal. The exact rate of increase varies with the size and hence with the weight of the baby.

A baby of short gestation has a relatively larger head than a full term baby. The average weights and head circumferences at birth are as follows:

	weight	head circumference
28 weeks	2 lb 4 oz (1·0 Kg.)	10 inches (25·5 cm.)
32 weeks	3 lb 8 oz (1·5 Kg.)	$11\frac{1}{2}$ inches (29 cm.)
36 weeks	5 lb 4 oz (2·4 Kg.)	$12\frac{3}{4}$ inches (32·5 cm.)
40 weeks	7 lb 8 oz (3·4 Kg.)	$13\frac{3}{4}$ inches (35 cm.)

The head size is related to the size of the baby as well as to his age. A big baby is likely to have a bigger head than a small baby of the same age and vice versa. The baby's weight is the easiest guide to his overall size. Consequently, when there is any doubt, the head circumference is plotted on the head circumference chart and the baby's weight on the weight chart. The two should correspond in their percentile

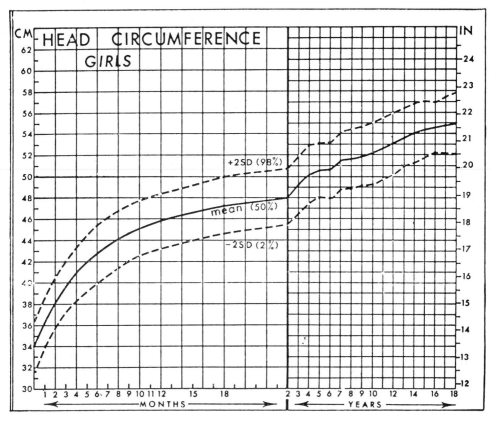

Fig. 1a.

HEAD CIRCUMFERENCE TABLE — GIRLS

| Age in Years | Percentiles | | | | | |
	10		50		90	
	In.	Cm.	In.	Cm.	In.	Cm.
0·25	15·0	38·1	15·6	39·7	16·1	40·9
0·50	16·2	41·2	16·9	42·9	17·4	44·2
0·75	17·0	43·2	17·6	44·6	18·1	46·2
1	17·5	44·4	18·0	45·7	18·6	47·2
2	18·1	46·2	18·9	48·0	19·4	49·3
3	18·5	47·1	19·4	49·2	19·9	50·5
4	18·9	48·0	19·6	49·9	20·2	51·4
5	19·1	48·6	19·8	50·4	20·4	51·9

3

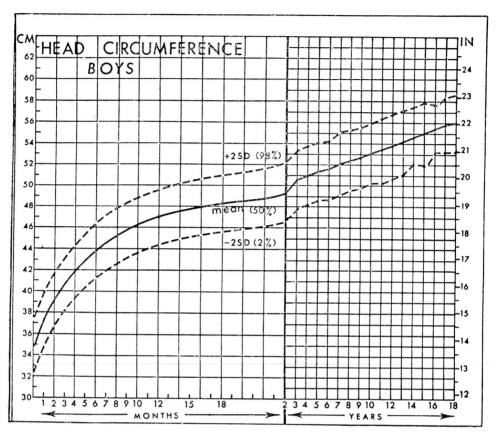

Fig. 1b.

HEAD CIRCUMFERENCE TABLE — BOYS

Age in Years	Percentiles					
	10		**50**		**90**	
	In.	Cm.	In.	Cm.	In.	Cm.
0·25	15·5	39·3	16·0	40·6	16·6	42·1
0·50	16·5	42·0	17·2	43·8	17·7	45·0
0·75	17·1	43·6	18·0	45·7	18·6	47·2
1	17·5	44·5	18·4	46·8	19·1	48·5
2	18·5	47·1	19·3	49·1	20·0	50·9
3	19·0	48·2	19·8	50·2	20·5	52·0
4	19·3	48·9	20·0	50·8	20·7	52·5
5	19·4	49·4	20·2	51·3	20·9	53·0

placing. A child's head circumference may be exactly on the 50th percentile for his age and yet, if he is a very small baby, he may have hydrocephalus or, if he is a big baby, microcephaly (Fig. 2a and b. Note that neither of these cases are severe.)

When the difference of the head circumference from the average expected for the child's age and weight has been calculated, the significance of this difference or deviation is evaluated by expressing the circumference in standard deviations from the mean. In head circumference a deviation from the mean of half an inch is about one standard deviation. A clinical impression of mental retardation is supported by finding that the head circumference is more than 2 S.D. i.e. more than one inch, above or below the mean.

Whenever a child has an unusually shaped or sized head, or odd face, one should look at the mother and father for a possible hereditary reason.

Hydrocephalus is suggested if the head circumference is increasing unusually fast. The rate of gain is best detected by charting successive measurements on a head circumference chart.

The commoner causes of an unusually small head for the child's age are as follows:—

        Small baby
        Familial feature
        Mental subnormality
        Craniostenosis

The commoner causes of an unusually large head for the child's age are as follows:—

        Large baby
        Familial feature
        Hydrocephalus
        Megalencephaly
        Hydranencephaly

An older child (e.g. 9 to 12 months) with a 'failure to thrive' syndrome, has a relatively large head.

Fig. 2a. Microcephalic head   **Fig. 2b. Hydrocephalic head**

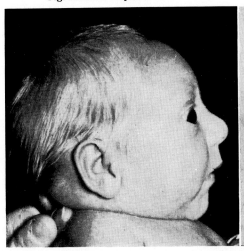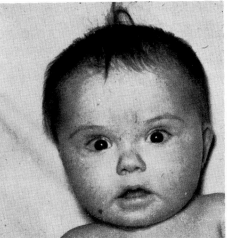

Examination of Muscles

1. *The consistency* of the muscles can be estimated by palpating, for example, the thighs or upper arms. In a hypotonic child they feel flabby.

2. *Muscle Tone* is defined as the resistance to passive movement when the segments of the limbs are moved by the examiner. Decreased resistance is hypotonia; increased resistance is hypertonia. The forearm can be extended and flexed at the elbow; the thighs (flexed to be at right angles with the trunk) abducted and adducted at the hips; the leg (with the thigh in the same position) flexed and extended at the knee. Examine also by flexing and extending the hand at the wrist and the foot at the ankle. Voluntary or involuntary muscular contraction may give increased resistance to passive movement but such resistance is inconstant and does not indicate continuing hypertonus.

3. *The range of movement* is assessed, especially of the thigh at the hip, the leg at the knee and the foot at the ankle. With hypotonia the range of movement is usually increased and with hypertonia it is usually decreased. In the hypotonic child the flexed thighs may abduct to lie flat on the couch. In the child with spastic hypertonia, when the thighs are at right angles to the trunk, there is commonly limitation of abduction of the thighs, of extension of leg at the knee, and of dorsiflexion of the foot at the ankle.

4. *Flapping the hand or foot* is carried out by holding the proximal segment of the limb and shaking the limb. In the hypotonic limb the range and duration of movement of the flapping hand or foot is increased; in the hypertonic they are decreased.

5. *Inspection of posture* gives information indicative of tone. In the child with spastic hypertonia, the lower limbs are often extended and adducted.

In all forms of cerebral palsy, whether the limbs are stiff or floppy, the muscles of the neck and trunk are weak and hypotonic. There is, therefore, excessive head lag when the child is pulled from the supine to the sitting position and when the child is placed in a sitting position the back is excessively rounded.

In athetoid cerebral palsy there may be intermittent arching of the back.

Hypertonia is nearly always evidence of an unusually brisk stretch reflex; it is commonly accompanied by unusually brisk tendon jerks and by ankle clonus.

Tendon Reflexes *

The knee jerk may be elicited by tapping over the patellar tendon (Fig. 3). When the knee jerk is examined, the thigh should be partly flexed at the hip and the leg partly flexed at the knee. Infants under 6 or 8 months may be examined when lying supine; older children when sitting. The examiner can also tap at intervals up the leg from the ankle until the knee is reached. A marked response when tapping over the lower part of the skin means that the knee jerk is unusually brisk, but not necessarily abnormal. In small infants the examiner may tap the patellar tendon with his finger.

The biceps jerk is often best tested by placing the forefinger on the biceps tendon at the elbow and another finger lightly on the forearm. When the forefinger is tapped by a pattellar hammer, the contraction can be felt with the other finger (Fig. 4).

---

* For fuller description of the neurological examination of children see Paine R.S. and Oppé T.E. (1966) Clinics in Dev. Med. 20/21. Spastics Soc. in association with William Heinemann Medical Books Ltd., London.

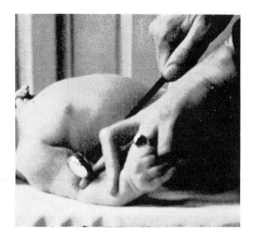

Fig. 4.

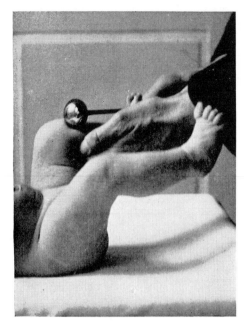

Fig. 3.

Other commonly elicited reflexes, such as the triceps, supinator and ankle jerks, are evoked as in the adult.

If the knee jerks are unusually brisk, there may be some degree of ankle clonus. This is tested for with the thigh partly flexed and abducted at the hip, and with the leg partly flexed at the knee. Gentle but rapid dorsiflexion of the foot with the index finger under the distal half of the sole may elicit clonus.

Discussion

Briskness or sluggishness of tendon responses or even sustained clonus by themselves, without other signs, such as delayed motor development, is of little significance; but asymmetry of response is, providing that the head was in the midline throughout the examination so that the tone in the limbs was not affected by the asymmetric tonic neck response.

Examination of the Hips for Dislocation and for Instability

Hart's test

With the baby lying on his back, legs towards the examiner, the lower limbs are first adducted and extended. The thighs — still adducted — are then flexed to right angles with the trunk. With the tips of the fore and middle fingers over the great trochanter and the leg held by the thumb around the knee (see Fig. 5), the thighs are abducted.

In the first week the thigh normally abducts to 90° from the midline. The normal range of abduction diminishes, but at 6 weeks, the thigh still usually abducts to at least 70° from the midline.

Interpretation. In the early weeks of life decreased abduction, whether unilateral or bilateral, is highly suggestive of subluxation of the hip joint. It may be difficult to

7

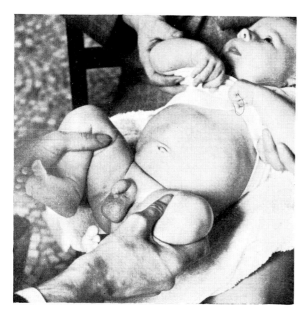

Fig. 5.

be certain whether abduction is normal or not but whenever there is doubt the child should be referred to a paediatrician or orthopaedic surgeon for further examination.

After the early weeks of life decreased abduction may indicate subluxation of the hips or it may indicate hypertonia or contracture of the thigh adductors due to spastic cerebral palsy. It may also indicate muscle contracture due to the child, usually mentally retarded, always lying in one position. It may also be due to coxa vara.

Barlow's modification of Ortolani's test

The baby is laid on his back as in Hart's test. The thighs and the knees are flexed to right angles. The examiner places the thumb of each hand on the inner side of the upper part of the infant's thighs and the middle fingers over the great trochanter (see Fig. 5). The thighs are then placed in mid abduction, at right angles to each other. The examiner then lifts the great trochanter of each hip in turn. This will quickly reveal a dislocation because, as this manoeuvre reduces a dislocation, the head of the femur being tested will be felt to slip into the acetabulum with a jerk (a better term than a 'click').

Dislocation is rare but instability of the hip is not. This usually resolves but as it may go on to dislocation it must be detected and the child referred to a hospital. If the absence of dislocation has been established by a normal Hart's test or the manoeuvre described in the first paragraph, instability is searched for. With the thumb, the head of the femur is pressed downwards and outwards and, in an unduly lax hip capsule, this will cause the head to be displaced out of the acetabulum. A jerk may be felt then or upon reversing the pressure to restore the head of the femur into the acetabulum.

Interpretation. Dislocation or instability revealed by Barlow's test is an indication for immediate referral to a paediatrician or orthopaedic surgeon.

Inherent Primitive and Secondary Responses in the First Year

The newborn full term infant adopts a 'fetal' position of general flexion of spine and limbs. When he moves his limbs, he tends to flex or extend them at all joints simultaneously. The normal infant comes to be able to flex one joint while another is extending; the spastic infant is often unable to do this till a much later age.

The normal newborn has a number of 'primitive' inherent responses many of which wane during the first 3 or 4 months. If any of these primitive responses, for example, the Moro or startle response, is absent in the neonatal period, it is a sign of disordered cerebral function. Similarly the persistence, after the age of 6 months, of a response which normally wanes by the age of 4 months, is also a sign of neurodevelopmental abnormality.

As the primitive responses wane, other inherent 'secondary' responses emerge. These are concerned with rolling, balancing and protection in falling.

The primitive responses include

1. Local: head: righting response
              upper limbs: primitive grasp of fingers
                            bringing arms forward when placed prone
              lower limbs: primitive grasp of toes
                            placing response of lower limbs
                            supporting
                            primary stepping

2. General: Asymmetric tonic neck
              response;   Moro response

The secondary responses include
         Rolling
         Balancing
         Protective reactions

Primitive Responses

Head righting response The newborn infant, held vertical, can momentarily keep his head balanced erect (Fig. 6). At 10 weeks, in ventral suspension he lifts his head so that the face is vertical and the mouth horizontal.

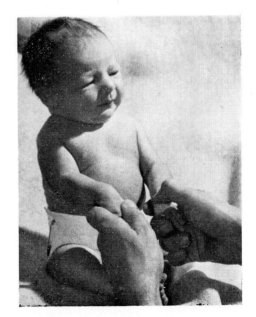

Fig. 6.

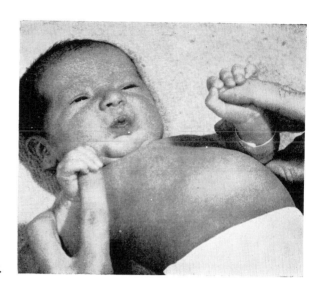

Fig. 7.

Finger grasp   For the first two months the hands are shut most of the time. The thumb is sometimes inside the fingers. If an object is placed in the palm, the fingers close on it, the gripping being reinforced if the object is pulled against the encircling fingers (Fig. 7). After the 2nd month persistent 'fisting' indicates delay in motor development. Fisting on one side suggests hemiplegia.

Fig. 8.

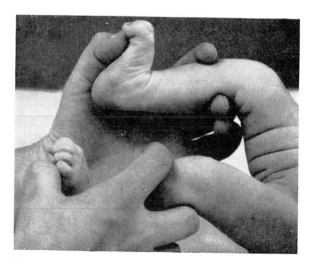

Toe grasp   Pressure on the sole at the base of the toes causes flexion of the toes, (Fig. 8). The toe grasp response normally persists until 9 to 12 months.

10

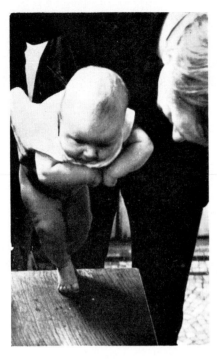

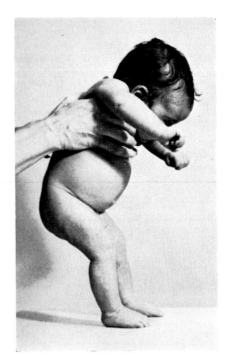

Fig. 9.   Fig. 10.

Placing response   The child is held vertical and the dorsum of the feet or front of the leg moved against the lower edge of the top of a table. The lower limb is flexed, swung forward and extended so that the child 'steps over the kerb' (Fig. 9). Response becomes less vigorous at 6 months but persists into the second year. The reaction is of value in detecting asymmetry of response between the two lower limbs. In a child of 5 or 6 months a poor placing with a vigorous supporting response suggests excessive extensor activity as is seen in the spastic child (Paine 1964)

Supporting response   The child is held erect and lowered so that the soles of the feet are in contact with the table top. In the first 3 to 4 months most infants extend the lower limbs and will support their weight. In the 4th, 5th and 6th months the response is less vigorous but from 6 months it is normally present again and persists (Fig. 10).

Primary stepping   The infant held erect and supporting his weight is then leant forward. During the first 6 weeks he will usually respond by stepping forward. Even after it has disappeared it may be evoked by passive extension of the head (Mac Keith 1964). The response is useful for demonstrating to the mother the functional efficiency of the lower limbs and for detecting asymmetry as in hemiplegia (Fig. 11a and b).

11

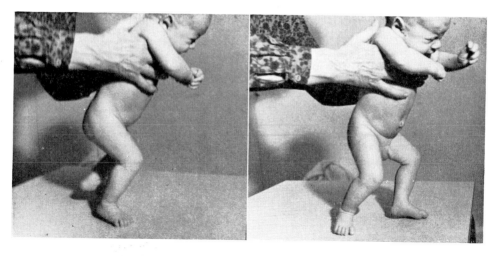

Fig. 11 *a* and *b*.

Asymmetric tonic neck response During the first 3 or 4 months when the infant's head turns to one side, the upper limbs take the fencer's position; the arm extends on the side to which the face is turned. The other arm is flexed. The lower limbs take a similar attitude to the upper limb on the same side. The trunk is concave to the occipital side. The ATNR is never an obligatory response but in the 3rd or 4th months the infant's limbs are in ATNR postures 50 per cent of the time (Fig. 12). If in the first month or two the infant keeps his head persistently turned to one side, there may be persisting fisting in the occipital hand (suggesting a hemiparesis), apparent shortening of the occipital lower limb and curvature of the spine. There may also be later delay in turning the head to sounds made on what was the occipital side of the head.

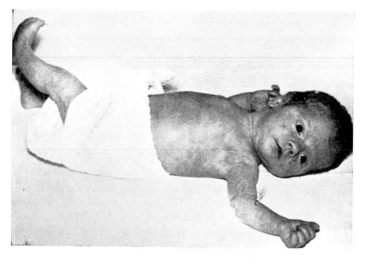

Fig. 12.

12

Moro response In the first 3 or 4 months, if the supine infant's head is allowed to drop as indicated in figures 13*a* and *b*, there is sudden extension and abduction of the upper limbs, with opening of the hands, followed by flexion to the midline (Fig. 13*a* and *b*). An asymmetrical Moro response may indicate an Erb's palsy or an injury of an upper limb.

Fig. 13*a* and *b*.

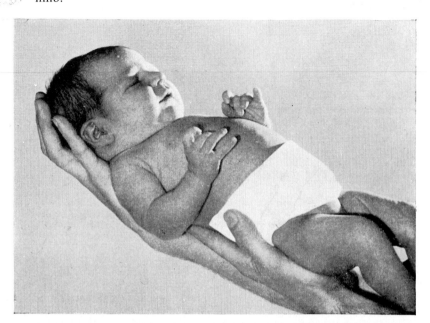

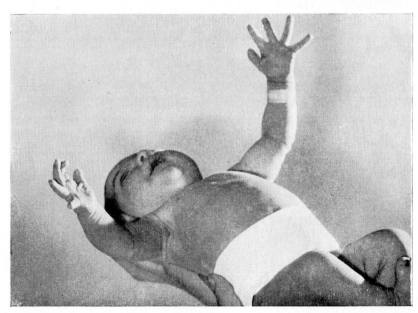

13

The tests on pages 14, 15 and 16 are not performed routinely as part of developmental screening, but a knowledge of them will increase the examiner's skills.

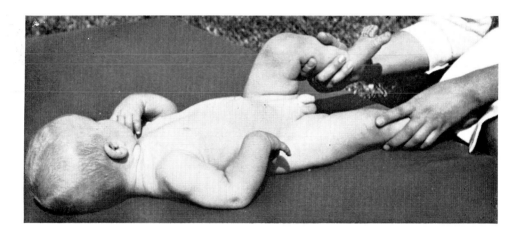

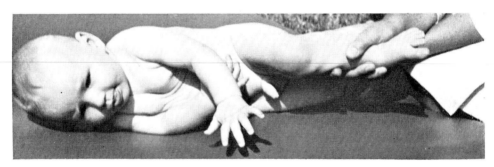

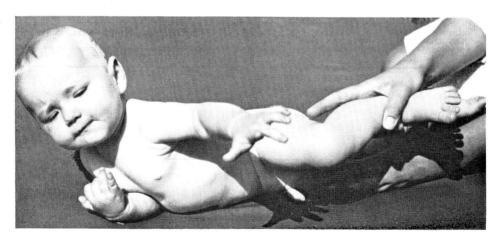

Fig. 14 *a*, *b* and *c*.

Secondary Responses

These appear at age 4 to 7 months and in some degree persist. That they are not learned but inherent can be demonstrated by evoking them before the baby has used them in voluntary activity.

Rolling Response

In the newborn period, if the baby's head is rotated the body tends to follow it around, rather like a log. As the child grows older, a complicated set of reactions can be observed as the child is rolled (Fig. 14). Derotative righting, well described by Milani-Comparetti and Gidoni (1967), begins to develop around the fourth month.

If the child is supine and the head is turned, first the hips and lower limbs turn into alignment and then the shoulders and thorax. These trunk-on-head and head-on-trunk righting responses are the basis for rolling.

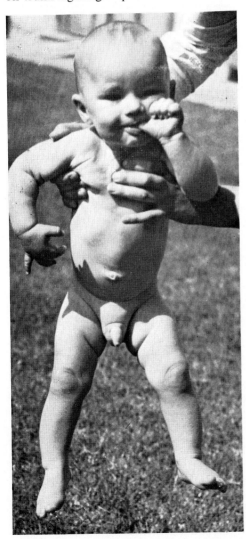

Fig. 15. The 'downward parachute' reaction, first seen at about the 4th month. The lower limbs extend and abduct as the baby is rapidly lowered towards the ground.

Balancing reactions These keep the head and body properly oriented in space; by them the head is 'righted' and the body comes into line with it. Sideways balance is tested by holding the child erect and tilting him to one side. At 4 months old he will tilt his head to 30° to keep his eyes level. At 5 months the spine curves to aid in the compensatory adjustment. But the baby who shows these reactions when held up and tilted does not use them when he is first placed in a sitting position.

Protective reactions These are also called propping, saving or parachute reactions. Balancing reactions are in the opposite direction to the displacing force; protective reactions are in the same direction. They appear in response to a sudden displacing force or when a slower force can no longer be compensated by balancing.

The 'forward parachute (or protective) reaction' is shown when an infant held vertically in the air is tilted towards the ground: the upper

Fig. 16a.

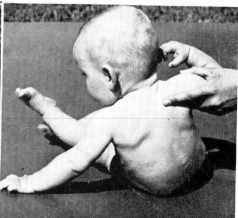

Fig. 16 b.

limbs and fingers abduct and extend (Fig. 16a). At 6 months, 30 per cent of infants show no response, 40 per cent a partial response and 30 per cent the full response. By 9 months most infants show the response. The sideways protective reaction is seen in the sitting position from the age of 6 or 8 months (Fig. 16b); the backward protective reaction from 10 or 12 months.

The child cannot walk until he has both balancing and protective reactions.

The time of disappearance of the primitive responses and appearance of the secondary responses shows wide variation and any interpretation of the significance of these responses should be in association with the rest of the developmental examination.

The Developmental Screening Examination

The Choice of Ages for Developmental Screening Examinations

The following key ages have been selected for the developmental screenings:

6 weeks
6 months
10 months
18 months
2 years
3 years
$4\frac{1}{2}$ years

Some of the above ages have been selected partly because it is easier to assess the progress of development in babies at these ages than at others. This applies particularly to the first three. It is easier to decide whether a child is performing normally for his age at 6 weeks or 6 months than at 3 or at 4 months, and at 6 or 10 months than at 8 months. The reason lies in the fact that shortly before 6 weeks, 6 months and 10 months, various important transitions occur.

The ages at which children usually attend child welfare or well baby clinics or their doctors for immunisation and other purposes, have also influenced the choice of these ages.

The Developmental History

The history taken when a child is seen must include developmental items because these give information on development in the interval since the previous screening examination (and hence on the rate of development) and because they make it possible to compare the mother's version of the child's skills with the results of the examiner's more objective examination.

Mother and examiner must understand what each other says. The questions are therefore put in a way which is understood and which elicits unambiguous answers. The examiner has also to assess the mother's ability to recall and to describe her child's performance. The record of the screening should specify whether an item recorded is reported by the mother or observed by the examiner himself. One way is to place a capital 'M' before statements of the mother and a capital 'E' before a record of the examiner's observation.

Developmental delays and the neurological disorders underlying them may present with disturbances of feeding, sleeping or activity. These symptoms may require careful interpretation. For example, poor coordination of sucking, difficulty in feeding from hyperexcitability or from a general lack of liveliness may stem from cerebral dysfunction (e.g. from perinatal brain injury), from disturbance of mother-baby relationship or from interaction between both of these. Physical illnesses in the child and in the mother may influence developmental progress and need to be known. Depression in the mother can also have an important effect on the child's progress.

17

The mother's doubts or anxieties about the child are often important early warnings and even when they are not associated with anything abnormal in the child they need to be explored and explained. The physical and social environment of the child can profoundly influence his development and must be known in order to assess the significance of the developmental observations. The child may have to be restrained from activity in his home; his mother may have no time for him; he may be in care of a succession of child minders. He may or may not, when older, have the stimulus of play with other children.

The details of the essential developmental history will be included in the sections which follow.

The Developmental Examination

It helps the doctor to see mother and child together and to see the mother handling her child. Usually the child will have been undressed outside to be weighed; it saves a considerable amount of the examiner's time if the child comes into his room wearing only his undergarments or a vest and napkin.

The order in which developmental features are elicited is based on convenience. In the case of the six-month-old baby, it would be wise to test his vision and give him bricks in order to test his manipulative development and then to test his hearing before further undressing or examining him in supine and prone; if these were done first he might be crying before the vision and manipulation and the hearing could be tested.

The small infant and often the toddler is most conveniently observed while he is on his mother's knee. At times it is convenient to test hearing in the infant under 6 months of age while he is lying supine on a couch or table. Sometimes it is best for the older child to be sitting or standing at a small table.

The child is closely observed for interest, alertness and responsiveness, and for the head shape and for any abnormality of the eyes (squint, nystagmus etc). He is then given a one inch cube, to test his vision and manipulation, and then his response to sound is tested. Only after this should he be completely undressed. Examination of the mouth (for which a spatula may be necessary) should be left to the last, for it is apt to lead to crying.

In the case of the toddler, one will observe his gait and his interest in his surroundings, and then his response to simple commands, before his mother sits him on her knee. He is then given suitable toys and one-inch cubes to play with.

Significance of Findings

The significance of individual abnormal findings varies, some being of greater importance than others. Some findings (for example a strabismus, even if intermittent, in a child aged 6 months or more) are significant even when found alone; others may not be of significance by themselves.

A combination of several abnormal findings always indicates a need for further study of the child. For example, a rather small head circumference (e.g. $1\frac{1}{2}$ S.D. below the mean for age and weight) would be noted but no action taken. A similarly small head in combination with delay in motor development or in smiling back would arouse much more anxiety.

In a similar way factors in the history influence the examiner's attitude to the finding of a possibly abnormal response. 'Risk factors' are incidents in the child's history which are potentially traumatic and increase his liability to have a handicap. If the child is clearly normal, their importance should not be exaggerated, but if the examiner is doubtful, he takes the risk factor into consideration. A child aged six months with a rather poor response to sounds but a clear history would be re-examined in one month, but if there was a history of rubella during the 3rd month of pregnancy, the child would be referred without delay for specialist examination (and his hearing would be re-examined at intervals for at least 5 years).

Interpretation therefore depends on

    i)   the particular abnormal finding or findings.

    ii)   the presence of a constellation of abnormal findings.

    iii)   the signs taken in conjunction with the history including any history of risk factors.

See also section on Interpretation, page 61.

Even when a child's hearing, vision and general development have been shown to be normal at, say, the age of six months, it remains essential to repeat the procedures at intervals over succeeding years to know whether at each age development in all fields continues to be normal.

Action to be Taken

At the end of each section describing the screening examination for each particular age, the important items which indicate a developmental delay or which may point to a specific abnormality are listed. The action to be taken by the examiner must depend on the degree of doubt which he feels about the developmental delay or the signs which he has elicited and about their significance. If his suspicion of abnormality is only slight, he may decide to see the child again after an interval of a week or a month. If the suspicion is greater or if a significant abnormality or a combination of risk factor plus suspicious finding is present, he will at once arrange for further assessment of the child. In the U.K. this will be by referring the child via the family doctor to a paediatric (or to a special assessment) clinic. In other countries the physician may feel competent to carry out the detailed comprehensive assessment himself or he may refer the child for more specialised help.

Telling the Parents

Just as a mother is commonly alarmed to hear that her baby is 'underweight' unless time is taken to explain to her that 50 per cent of infants have weights below the average for their age, so a mother can easily be made unnecessarily anxious about her child's development. There is considerable variation of development which falls within the range of normal. If the examiner finds a delay which he is satisfied is within the range of normal and is not significant, then he should not mention it to the mother. If the examiner wishes to re-examine after a short interval, he may speak of 'doing the rest of the test in 4 weeks time'. If he decides that the child should be referred to a specialist he will explain that this is done so that if there is any developmental delay, the child can have early treatment.

19

Equipment

It is more pleasant to work in a light, airy room which is used solely for clinic work or for the examination of children, but frequently it may be necessary for the doctor to use a room which is required for other purposes at other times, or to conduct his clinic in a church hall or some other community house which is less than ideal. In these circumstances it is essential to use screens to divide up the available space and to give a measure of privacy for examinations and interviews. The room must be warm enough for the baby to be undressed without discomfort.

Apart from the doctor's own writing table and chairs for the parents, the basic equipment should include an examination table for babies and young children, a nursery table and chair and a soft foam rubber floor mat for children to sit on.

The examination table should be about 3 feet high, with a rim around it (Fig. 17a); it should be remembered that, from about 4 months, the baby can roll over. The mattress on the table should preferably be of the soft 'kapok' type rather than foam rubber, so that a depression can be made for the baby's head to rest in. It should be covered with a waterproof material, then with a large sheet, tucked in, which can be removed during the session as 'accidents' occur.

Testing Material and Toys

It is best if all toys are kept in a box, with only one or two at most put on the low table for the toddler. Toys used for testing should be brought out singly by the examiner and immediately replaced. The child's attention must be focussed on the task presented to him; if a number of toys are put out he is apt to be distracted by them.

For a baby under 6 or 7 months, a variety of sound-making toys are used for tests of hearing. A suspended ball or ring, and sugar pellets will be useful for testing vision. A set of balls of graduated sizes is being developed for testing visual acuity of children from the age of 9 months (Sheridan 1969).

For the child from 6 months onwards, 1 inch cubes form an invaluable part of the equipment. Ordinary wooden bricks of this size are quite adequate but may prove difficult to keep sterile; solid plastic ones are better but more difficult to obtain. Hollow plastic bricks, because of their light weight, can be difficult for the young child to handle.

From 12 months to two years the child may be too sophisticated to respond to standard tests of hearing with sound-making toys, and other means have to be devised to assess the child's understanding of speech. One should have a variety of familiar objects which the child can define by use, give on request by name or identify in single words. Examples of objects are shown in the foreground in Fig. 17 c.

By two and a half years the child can show the meaning he has found in the world around him in his spontaneous play with doll's house furniture. A simple picture book will help in demonstrating comprehension of pictures and, in slightly older children, stimulate conversation.

STYCAR tests for hearing and vision from two years onwards are detailed on page 65.

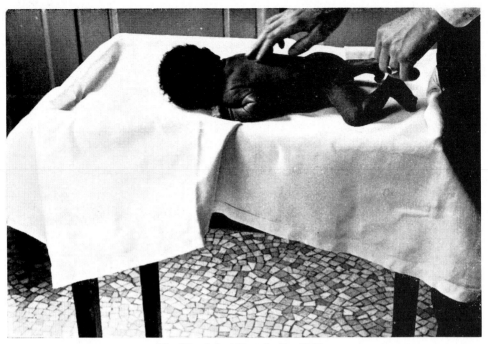

Fig. 17 *a*. Infant Examination Table.

Fig. 17 *b*. Suggested equipment for testing up to 10 months.

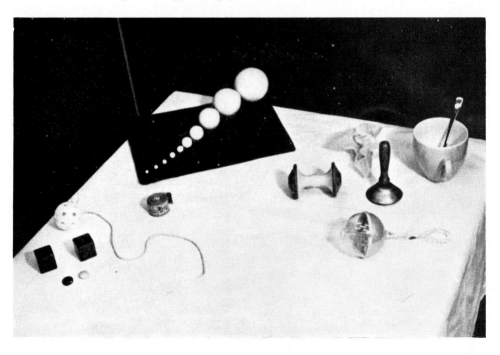

Fig. 17 *c* and *d*. Suggested equipment for testing (*above*) up to 2 years and (*below*) up to 5 years.

The Six-week-old Baby

Between birth and six weeks of age the normal baby becomes aware of sensory stimuli from the outside world and begins to assimilate these sensations. By six weeks of age, reception of these sensory stimuli is assisted by the beginning of control of the head position. When the baby is raised to the sitting position the head lag is by no means as complete as at an earlier age. In the prone lying and ventral suspension positions a 'righting' reaction of the head is seen whereby the head is raised, at least momentarily, to a forward looking position.

He shows response to visual stimuli by visually fixing upon nearby objects and by following them if they are moved before his face from side to side over a limited range.

Response to auditory stimuli may be shown by a startle response, by stilling, by opening the eyes wider, a catch in the respiration, blinking, crying or grimacing.

By six weeks of age the baby begins to show some adaptive social behaviour in response to stimuli, the most marked being the visual fixing especially on the human face and the smiling back in response to the mother's overtures (Fig. 18).

The General History

How is he getting on?

Does he take his feeds well, sleep well, keep contented?

Is there anything which you would like to ask me about him?

Fig. 18.

23

Symptoms about which one does not specifically enquire, but which call for further questioning if they are mentioned by the mother.

1. Inco-ordination of sucking and swallowing, and difficulty with the use of the tongue. At this age, the mother's impression of inefficiency may be of no significance. If the incoordination is definite and if it is associated with other signs, it may be a sign of mental subnormality or of pseudo bulbar palsy and/or cerebral palsy.

2. Undue sleepiness. This is commonly of no significance, representing nothing more than immaturity. If associated with other signs, it *could* be due to mental subnormality.

3. Excessive irritability, constant crying. This is not usually a sign of physical abnormality. The child may cry because he is hungry, because he needs to be picked up and cuddled or to be propped up so that he can look around. It may also be associated with maternal insecurity. It may be an early manifestation of his inherent personality. Mothers with young babies should be enjoying them and persistent or recurrent crying should be gone into thoroughly and every effort made to help without delay. *Rarely*, persistent crying is evidence of metabolic disorder, glaucoma or other serious disorder.

4. General home conditions associated with undue difficulty for the mother or child.

Developmental History

Proper allowance must be made for short gestation. If the infant were born, say four weeks prematurely, he has missed four weeks development in utero. Instead of beginning to smile at 4 to 6 weeks, he would be expected to smile at 4 to 6 weeks *plus* 4, i.e. 8 to 10 weeks.

Motor Function

Does he move his limbs actively and equally?

Eye Fixation

'Does he watch you intently when you are feeding him or speaking to him?' This 'regard' precedes the social smile.

Vocalisation

Has he begun to coo or to make other little noises? These are commonly evoked by the mother's talking to the child. Vocalisation with smiles begins usually a week or two after the first appearance of the social smile.

Social behaviour

Smile: Has he begun to smile back at you when you talk to him?

It is essential to ensure that the mother understands that you refer to a definite *smile in response to social overture*. She is apt to regard any facial movement in sleep as a smile. Some mothers have the idea that babies smile only if they experience pain from wind; others that babies cannot see before the age of six weeks.

A normal baby may exceptionally begin to smile in response to social overture at 3 or 4 days of age; the usual age at which he begins to smile is 4 to 6 weeks; but if a full term baby has not begun to smile by the age of 8 weeks, there is serious ground for concern.

General Inspection

(The outer clothes will have been removed in the waiting room). The doctor notices at a glance whether the baby, if awake, is alert and interested in his surroundings, and the mother's responsiveness to him.

The doctor also notices the size and shape of the skull and palpates the anterior fontanelle. Some degree of asymmetry of the skull is common. The occiput is often flattened on one side because in the early months the child persistently turns the face to that side (Fig. 19). This postural asymmetry or postural plagiocephaly begins to resolve from the age of two months when the child comes to keep his head in the midline, and especially when he comes to sit, as there is then no longer such continuous pressure on the occiput on one side. The head circumference is measured at this stage, or at the end of the examination.

The mentally subnormal child may have a skull which is average in its overall circumference, but whose shape may indicate possible abnormality; for example, the skull of a defective child often tapers off towards the vertex; sometimes, as in Down's Syndrome (mongolism) the occiput is flat.

If there is any doubt as to whether the fontanelle is bulging or not, one will also palpate the sutures for undue separation. If there is any suspicion of craniostenosis, one will palpate the sutures for the characteristic ridging.

Fig. 19. Asymmetry of skull: note prominence of right brow and flattening of right occiput.

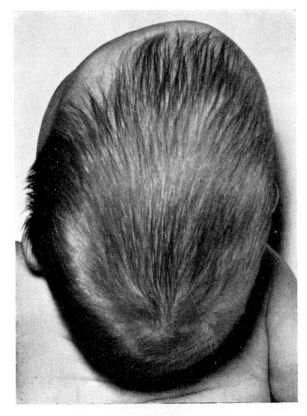

The general examination must include the body weight, head circumference, examinations of the hips, femoral pulses, genitalia and tendon reflexes. These will conveniently be done later when the child is seen undressed in the supine position.

THE CHILD'S NAPKIN MUST ALWAYS BE REMOVED.

Watch the mother and baby.

Where possible the doctor should confirm the mother's story of her child's achievements in various fields by his own observation. This is not always possible; the child may be asleep, or having been aroused from his sleep, may be crying. Hence the baby should be observed before the mother removes the vest and napkin, for he may cry when undressed. If the baby is awake, his visual and auditory 'alertness' may be observed (Fig. 20).

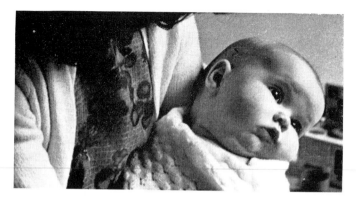

Fig. 20.

Posture and Gross Motor Performance

Supine Position

(On his mother's lap or preferably on the examination table or both). The examiner observes the posture of the baby. At six weeks the normal full term baby lies on his back with his elbows flexed and knees and hips partly flexed (Fig. 21). The doctor observes the amount and symmetry of movement.

If the child moves the limbs of one side less, he may have hemiplegia, or an injury to a humerus or to the brachial plexus (Erb's palsy) of that side. In a baby with persistent

Fig. 21.

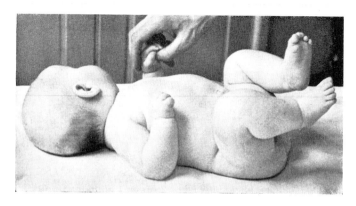

head turning to one side, the occipital limbs may be persistently flexed and appear to move less than the limbs on the side towards which the head is turned.

The infant who, when supine, lies with his lower limbs unduly extended may have spastic quadriplegia. The severely spastic child also tends to be relatively immobile. The child with excessive extensor tone regains a fetal position of flexion when he is asleep.

Head Control

Pulled to the sitting position the six-week-old infant shows considerable head lag, but he does help momentarily to raise his head, certainly when half pulled up, i.e. when the long axis of his body is at an angle of 45° to the couch. (Figs. 22a and b.)

 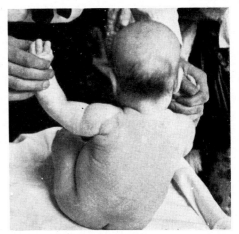

Fig. 22 *a* and *b*.

Prone Position

If the six-week-old baby is asleep, he reverts to the fetal position, with the pelvis high and the knees drawn up under his abdomen.

When he is awake, his pelvis is fairly low on the couch and his hips partly or intermittently extended (Fig. 23). (In this position the doctor glances down the

Fig. 23.

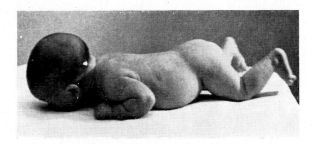

27

whole of the back for a congenital dermal sinus, or a tuft of hair which may point to a minute sinus, or other abnormality. A dermal sinus is only significant if one cannot see the bottom of it or if there are any neurological signs).

The child with his pelvis too high off the couch or with his knees under his abdomen when awake has developmental delay.

A child may appear to be unusually advanced in ventral suspension or in the prone position, because of excessive extensor tone in the erector spinal muscles. Such a child will, however, when pulled from supine to sitting, show excessive head lag. Discrepancy between performance in the prone and supine positions may indicate developmental abnormality; it occurs, for example, in cerebral palsy.

Ventral Suspension

The child is held with a hand under his abdomen.

The normal 6 week old baby in this position can momentarily hold his head up in the same plane as the rest of the body. He flexes his elbows, partly extends the hips and partly flexes the knees. (Fig. 24.)

The spastic or mentally subnormal child usually cannot hold his head up as far as the normal child can, and his arms and legs tend to hang down limply.

A child with cerebral palsy may show increased extensor tone in the muscles of the spine. This simulates an unusually advanced stage of motor development. Such increased extensor tone in neck and trunk muscles is usually intermittent.

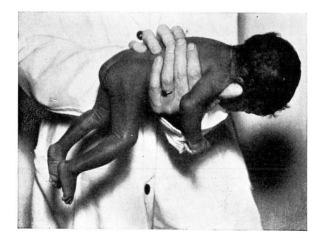

Fig. 24.

Vision

It is often easier to test for vision (and hearing) when the child is lying supine because the child finds it easier to turn the head. It may be obvious that the baby is watching the mother, and not merely responding to sound. The vision may be tested by moving an object (such as a dangling ring or ball (Fig. 25), a toy, or a patellar hammer) slowly across his line of vision at 9 to 12 inches (20 to 30 cms.) from the child's face.

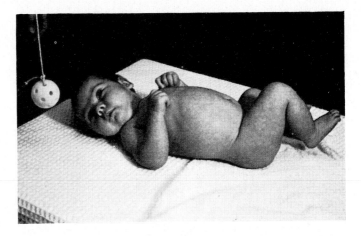

Fig. 25.

If the examiner stands holding the baby upright, facing the window, and then slowly turns with the baby towards the darker side of the room, the baby usually turns his head to keep his face towards the window.

If his eyes remain resolutely closed, he will often open them if he is held facing the examiner, and swung round. Attempts to force the eyelids open are usually unsatisfactory and lead him to close them tighter. If the child does not fixate and follow, the pupil reactions to light are tested. At this age a gross defect such as a cataract or a coloboma of the iris or nystagmus can be detected.

Hearing and Language

Response to nearby everyday sounds is usually inconsistent at this age, but should be looked for, particularly the response to the nearby mother's voice when she is out of the child's visual range. The child may quieten, blink, startle or cry when he hears a sound, loud or quiet; the eyes may move in the direction of the sound (Fig. 26). Note should be made of any response observed. If there is a strong 'at risk' history, e.g. of maternal rubella, the response to sounds should be observed at 6 weeks and at intervals thereafter.

Fig. 26.

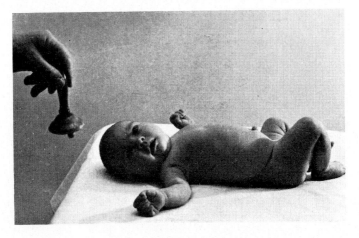

29

Vocalisation

The child cries; he may coo, and he may respond with vocalisations or even with laughter to the mother's advances.

Everyday Skills and Social Responses

The examiner may see the infant smiling back at the mother. He asks the mother to evoke a social smile and vocalisation.

Significance of Findings

Single suspicious signs, such as minor variations in head lag on pulling to sitting or in height of pelvis when prone, indicate the need for re-examination in a month. The following findings make referral to a specialist advisable:—

Any major anxiety in the mother

Restricted abduction of the hip

Unusually large or small head in relation to the weight, unless it is a familial feature.

Retardation in motor development (e.g. excessive head lag on pulling to the sitting position and pelvis too high in the prone position when awake).

Asymmetry of movements.

Marked hypotonia or hypertonia; asymmetry of tone; asymmetry of tendon jerks.

Development delay in visual response and also cataract, nystagmus or other disorder of the eyes.

Any definite developmental delay, including delay attributed to social deprivation.

Some items in the general history and examination, e.g. fits or cataracts, will both indicate need for expert further assessment and raise concern about the child's developmental progress.

In general, children suspected of abnormality are referred in the first place to a paediatric clinic. This may be for confirmation of the developmental delay, or for the comprehensive assessment that any developmentally retarded and hence handicapped child requires or, as in the case of fits, cataract etc., to have an expert check on possible causes of the disorder. When a child is referred direct to an ophthalmologist or orthopaedic surgeon, it is in general useful and wise also to ask a paediatrician to see the child.

The Six-month-old Baby

The six-month-old baby has developed remarkably since the early weeks of life. Most of the primary automatic responses have gone and some definitive capacities have emerged. The child now makes a social response to a stranger (Fig. 27).

The head is firmly controlled on the shoulders and the child turns it readily as he tries to locate visual and auditory stimuli. He enjoys being in the supported sitting position because this increases his range of vision and enables him to use his hands freely in play and exploration. He is usually still unable to sit alone on a firm surface with the legs extended at the knees. In the prone position he raises his head and chest off the couch and takes advantage of this position to learn more about his environment. At 4 to 5 months he is beginning to roll over, at first from prone to supine and then also in the reverse direction.

Visual fixation and following are well developed by now and, as conjugate movements should be well developed, strabismus, whether intermittent or persistent, cannot be accepted as an innocent feature. In addition to the ability to fixate objects visually the child can reach out and take them in a palmar grasp. By six months of age co-ordination of the two hands is developing and transfer of objects from hand to hand is beginning.

Fig. 27.

31

Interest in sound production is considerable, both of external sounds and his own voice, and razzing and babbling are frequently heard. He is beginning to chew.

He has for some time become excited when he sees food approaching. He protests if a toy is taken away and he holds his hands out to be picked up.

The General History

How is he getting on?
Is he eating well, sleeping well and is he contented?
Is there anything which you would like to ask me about him?

Developmental History

(Allowance must be made for short gestation, as before).

Motor
Does he sit well on the floor?

Vision
How long has he been reaching out and getting things without their being put in his hand? (Usually at age 5 months).

It is not always easy to obtain a reliable answer to this question. The mother is apt to say that he reached out and took objects at 3 or 4 months, when in fact he would only grasp an object if it was placed in his hand; he would play with a rattle placed in the hand, but could not pick it up if he dropped it onto the table in front of him. If he has not begun to reach out and get toys, one would ask how long he has been able to play with a rattle placed in his hand (usually at age 3 - 4 months).

Hearing
Does he turn his head when he hears sounds? When did he begin to do this? (Usually at age 3 - 4 months).

Vocalisations
Is he cooing and humming and, apart from crying at times, making quite a lot of noises?

Can he chew solid food e.g. a piece of apple or lumps in food? (Add 'I don't mean just sucking them'). It is not always easy to obtain a satisfactory answer to this question. Mothers may not realise that the ability to chew is not related to the presence of erupted teeth. Provided the infant has been given the opportunity to learn, the emergence at 6 or 7 months of the ability to chew solid food is probably correlated with normal intelligence and delay after the age of 10 months is suggestive of mental handicap.

Everyday skills and social responses
How much is he smiling and laughing?
The severely defective child may be smiling very little at this age.
Does he copy you in anything that you do? When did he begin?
Copying usually begins at 6 to 7 months. He may imitate a cough, or patting

the table. One has to assess the reliability of the mother's story by the nature of her reply.

Does he make any effort to attract your attention (e.g. by coughing etc.)? Usually begins about 7 months.

General Inspection

(1) One notices immediately the baby's *alertness* and interest in his surroundings and his *responsiveness* to his mother.

(2) The size and shape of *his head.*

(3) *Eyes:* One notices a strabismus, nystagmus (which suggests a serious visual defect), or cataract and observes whether he looks at and fixates faces and objects.

(4) *The Hands:* One notices whether the hands are predominantly open (as they usually are after 3 or 4 months), or tightly closed (as in a spastic child). In a hemiplegic child one hand is tightly closed, while the other is open.

The *general examination* includes the body weight, measurement of head circumference, examination of the hips and the tendon reflexes. The finding of ankle clonus at this age is much more significant than it is in a 6 week old baby, though even at this age it does not necessarily indicate organic disease. If the possibility of phenylketonuria arises from the presence of fits, retardation or eczema, the child is referred to a paediatrician.

Posture and Gross Motor Performance

When the child is *supine*, note the symmetry of movement. 'Hand regard' (which starts at 3 or 4 months) should have ceased by this age. (The child, when awake and lying on his back, holds his hands in front of his eyes, pronating and supinating them at the wrists. It is a feature of the 12 to 20 week baby, but is usually abnormal if it occurs after the age of 5 months. There is, however, a more mature purposeful watching, usually of one hand and forearm moved to and from the eyes, which may be seen up to the age of 9 or 10 months when the child, lying supine, has nothing else to do.)

Muscle Tone

This is tested as before. In an apparently normal baby, it is sufficient to test the range of abduction of the flexed thigh (as is done in examining for subluxation of the hips), of extension of the leg on the thigh flexed at right angles to the trunk and of dorsiflexion of the foot at the ankle.

Pulling to the sitting position

If the child is not able to sit, the doctor pulls him by his hands from the supine to the sitting position, assessing head lag if any, and head wobble (when he is swayed from side to side in the sitting position). Considerable head wobble at six months indicates poor head control. At 5 months old, when pulled forward, the normal child usually braces his shoulders and tends to flex his upper limbs at the elbow. He should be able to take his weight on his feet (Fig. 28 *a* and *b*).

The child who has the spastic form of cerebral palsy may also rise to his feet when pulled to the sitting position, because of the excessive extensor tone in his lower limbs. When such a child is pulled to the sitting position and not allowed to stand

Fig. 28 *a* and *b*.

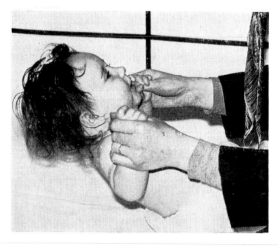

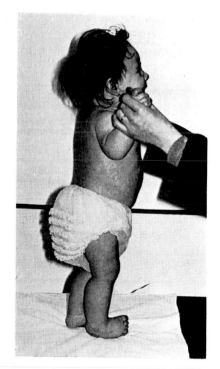

there may be marked flexion of the knees and a hand in the popliteal space can feel the spasm of the hamstrings. The child is likely to fall backwards from the sitting position, because of the spasm of the glutei which extends the thighs at the hips.

Sitting

The 6 months old baby can usually sit for a few minutes on a firm surface, such as the floor, with legs flexed and with the hands forward as props for support (Fig. 29).

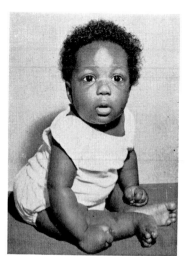

Fig. 29.

34

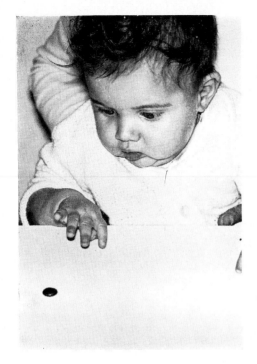

Fig. 30.   Fig. 31.

Supporting

The average 6 months old baby can bear most of the weight on the legs, provided only that the mother has allowed him to do so.

Prone position

This need not be tested routinely if the child is able to sit unsupported. By the age of 5 to 6 months, the child in the prone position is usually able to support his weight on the hands with extended arms.

Vision and Fine Manipulation

The baby lying on a couch follows an object such as a dangled ring or a patellar hammer from one side of the couch to the other (i.e. over an arc of 180°), following it upwards and downwards, converging on a near object. When sitting, he should look at a pellet; a pellet of paper or a small sweet can be used, placed on the table as in Fig. 30, or held out on the mother's or examiner's palm. (See also Sheridan, 1960.)

Manipulation

One places a one inch cube on the table within reach, and observes whether the child grasps it and how mature his grasp is (Fig. 31). The five-month baby grasps the cube in the palm of the hand. It is an insecure grasp and the cube soon slips from his hand. By 6 months the grasp is more secure. Transfer from one hand to the other begins at this age and should be noted. (Observe whether he uses *both* hands normally, i.e. has not a hemiplegia).

35

Hearing and Language

At this age a test of hearing must be carried out on all babies as a routine. The test sound should be made at a distance of 18″ from the ear, on a level with the ear, but slightly behind him so that he does not see the test object. The child may turn towards a bell or paper because he has *seen* it move.

Test sounds include vocalised ps, phth (for high pitch) and Ooo for low pitch, taking care not to blow on his ear (Fig. 32 *a*, *b* and *c*.) Other suitable sounds are produced by the crinkling of crisp thin, (e.g. toilet) paper, shaking a high-pitched rattle, or by stroking a spoon gently round the inside of a cup (Fig. 33). (For details of hearing testing at this and at later ages, see the papers by Mary Sheridan (1958, 1964) and the manual of the STYCAR hearing box. See page 65).

Fig. 32 *a*, *b* and *c* **(opposite)**
'Ps' test for hearing.

Fig. 33.

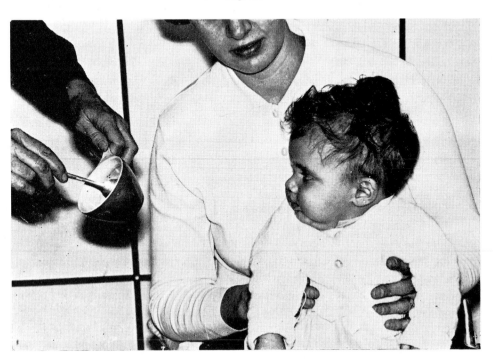

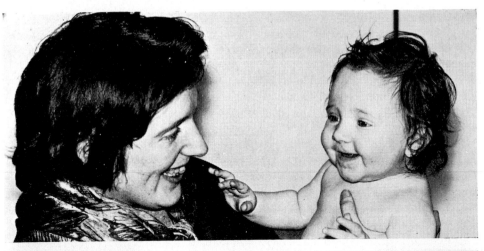

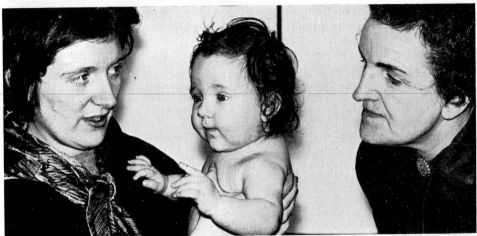

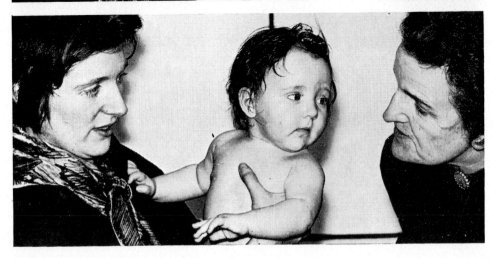

37

Vocalisation

The examiner may observe cooing or humming or other sounds. He may ask the mother to evoke vocalised responses from the child.. He will observe whether the vocalisations show cadences.

Everyday Skills and Social Responses

See page 32 under Developmental History.

Significance of Findings

A *possible* delay in motor, visual, auditory or social development or other doubt-ful signs, should be an indication to see the child again in a month; it is especially important to establish by the age of 7 or 8 months that hearing is normal (or defective).

It would be wise to refer a child to a specialist if there is:

Any major anxiety in the mother.

Limited abduction of hip.

Head circumference significantly small in relation to age and weight (more than 2 standard deviations below the mean).

Definite retardation in motor development.

Abnormal posture of hands or limbs, undue hypotonia or hypertonia, asymmetry of tone, ankle clonus or tendon reflexes.

Failure to fixate visually or presence of squint, nystagmus, cataract or other disorder of the eyes.

Failure to turn to sounds.

Little smiling or laughing or poor response to people or objects, if persistent from history.

Any definite developmental delay including delay attributed to social deprivation.

The Ten-month-old Baby

The ten-month-old baby is usually mobile, as he is able to roll actively on the floor, and often able to crawl and pull up to standing. These abilities widen his environment which is further extended by his own increasing exploration of his surroundings with his eyes, ears and hands. From 5 or 6 months of age he has been manipulating objects and from 9 months his manipulative abilities have improved greatly and he explores both the actions and the parts of objects. This manipulative exploration is aided by the development of a mature prehensile grasp between the tip of the index finger and the thumb and by the use of the index finger to explore. From eight months of age he will look to follow fallen objects.

His localisation of sounds is well developed, he shows a wide range of vocalisation and by this stage often imitates familiar sounds. He is certainly aware of much that is going on in his near environment and shows this by easy social responsiveness. Beginning awareness of differences between individuals and of his own ability to control his responses is seen in the occasional hesitation and inhibition of response to strangers.

The General History

How is he getting on?

Is there anything which you would like to ask me about him?

Developmental History

(The usual allowance must be made for short gestation).

Motor

When was he able to sit for a few seconds on the floor without support? (Usually by 7 months).

Is he able to crawl on his hands and knees—'creeping' in USA parlance (Fig. 34)? If so, when did he begin? (Usually around 10 months if he is going to crawl).

One has to distinguish crawling on the belly (usual age of achievement 9 months), in which the child pulls himself forward by his hands, from crawling on hands and knees ('creeping' in USA parlance) and from 'bear walking' which is done on hands and feet. Not all infants crawl. Some travel about sitting on their bottoms, a method sometimes called hitching or bottom-shuffling.

Can he pull himself up to the standing position in the playpen (Fig. 35), or in front of a chair? (Usual age, 9 months). If so, at what age did he begin?

Does he walk, holding on to the furniture? At what age did he begin to do this? (Usual age 10 months).

Everyday skills and social responses

Does he help you to dress him? i.e. does he hold his arm out for a coat, foot out for a shoe, or transfer an object from one hand to another in order to put an arm

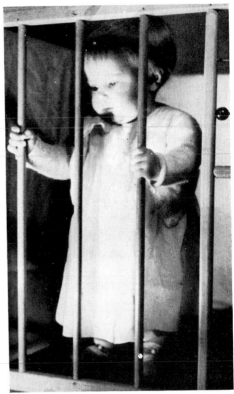

Fig. 35.

Fig. 34.

through the sleeve (usual age 9 - 10 months). At what age did he begin? This skill implies understanding, memory and imitation and is a valuable index of his level of development and ability to integrate his abilities. The child does not usually put his own clothes on until he is a good deal older.

Does he play games like pat-a-cake (clap hands)? (Usually by age 9 - 10 months).
Does he 'babble' while he plays?
Does he wave bye-bye? (Usual age 9 - 10 months). At what age did he begin?
Is he chewing solid food? (Usual age 6 months). At what age did he begin?
Is he feeding himself with a biscuit without help? (Usual age 9 months). At what age did he begin? Does he like to hold a spoon and can he manage to use it? (Using a spoon to feed himself is usually achieved by age 15 months).

General Inspection

This will include bodyweight, head circumference, abduction of thighs, tendon reflexes and, if in doubt, ankle clonus.

The child's interest in his surroundings, his alertness and his responsiveness to his mother and to other people are noted.

40

Fig. 36.

Posture and Gross Motor Performance

At 10 months babies are often unhappy if displaced from sitting to lying supine.

Observe the child's steadiness in the sitting position, on a firm surface (Fig. 36). Babies usually sit steadily by 8 months, but the child will be unlikely to be able to rotate in the sitting position to search for something behind him until he is 9 or 10 months old.

Observe for protective responses, i.e. the sitting child putting his arm to the side or in front of him for support when he leans over (present at 10 months).

Place him in the prone position and observe whether he adopts the crawling on hands and knees position (usual age 10 months).

He may be seen rising from the prone to the sitting position.

Observe whether the child stands on the floor, holding on or with support, bearing full weight on the legs.

Lower limbs

Examine for limitation in range of movements at the joints of the lower limbs. Test the abduction of the thighs flexed at the hips. With the thigh still at right angles to the trunk see if the leg can be extended at the knee almost to $180°$. Test the dorsiflexion of the foot at the ankle, usually to less than $90°$ between the shin and dorsum of the foot. (These are tests for tone and for contractures in thigh adductors, ham strings and calf muscles and are especially useful if standing is delayed).

Vision and Fine Manipulation

Note any visual following of an object in all directions (Fig. 37), whether he sees (and fixates or takes) a pellet of paper and also his quickness in glancing from one object to another. The 'rolling balls' test (Sheridan 1969) is useful at this age.

Note any strabismus; nystagmus suggests a serious defect of vision.

41

Fig. 37.

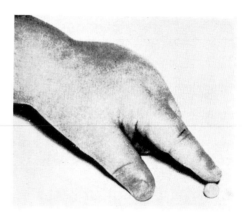

Fig. 38.

Manipulation

Look for the index finger approach (Fig. 38) to an object such as a cube (usually at age 10 months), and mature finger-thumb apposition (usually at 10 months). This means that the child can pick up a small pellet of paper between the *tip* of index finger and the *tip* of the thumb. The younger child starts by picking up the object in the palm of the hand, and then advances to doing so between the side of the thumb and the side of the index finger and only later achieves precise mature finger-tip—thumb-tip prehension.

When he is given two one inch cubes, watch for 'matching' — the baby bringing one cube up to the side of the other and apparently comparing the two (Fig. 39).

As before, the doctor notices whether the child uses both hands normally. He gets the child to prehend with each hand separately, so that he does not miss a hemiplegia. He observes, furthermore, if there is ataxia or tremor as the child reaches for the brick.

The child may offer a toy if the examiner's hand is held out to him, but he is unlikely to release it.

Fig. 39.

Hearing and Language

Test as before, 3 feet from the ear but out of sight, with the voiced sounds Ps, Phth, Ooo and his name. If the child fails to respond to voice sounds, observe his response to rustled paper, spoon on cup, rattle. At 7 to 8 months a child is expected to turn his head consistently to locate sounds on a level with or below his ear (Fig. 40) and 2 or 3 weeks later, above ear level. Ability to localise often occurs in one ear a week or so earlier than in the other.

Vocalisation: at 10 months a child usually babbles in long, tuneful chains of syllables. In a deaf child, vocalisation decreases as the factor of imitation enters.

Fig. 40

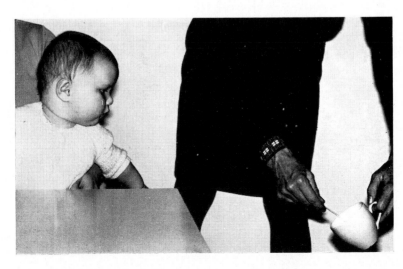

Everyday Skills and Social Responses

See page 39 under Developmental History. If possible, confirm mother's statements.

Significance of Findings

Doubt in the examiner's mind about the child's developmental progress is an indication to repeat the tests in 2 or 4 weeks' time.

It would be wise to refer the baby to a specialist for any of the following signs:

Any major anxiety in the mother.

A history of convulsions.

Significant eczema.

Head circumference significantly small in relation to age and body weight (more than 2 standard deviations below the mean).

Failure to bear reasonable weight on the legs.

Limitation of range of abduction of the thigh flexed at the hip joint, or extension of leg on thigh or of foot at ankle, on one or on both sides.

Abnormal static or mobile posture of hands or limbs.

Undue hypertonia, or hypotonia, asymmetry of tone, the presence of ankle clonus or of exaggerated tendon reflexes.

Doubt about visual response, strabismus, nystagmus.

Backwardness in manipulation.

Ataxia in reaching out for objects.

Failure to respond to sound, or decreased vocalisation (vocalisation decreases in deaf children from 6 or 8 months).

Failure to chew lumpy food.

Absence of smiling or laughing.

Any definite delay in development, including delay attributed to social deprivation.

The Eighteen-month-old Child

One thinks of the eighteen-month-old child as being a toddler, but some norma children are still not walking independently at this age. However, the child is usually highly active, often unsteady, with a lively response to all the objects around him, and is beginning to show some constructive activity, for example by building two or three cubes into a tower, or putting a lid onto a box. Verbal comprehension is well marked at this stage and it is usual to hear him produce a number of familiar words. The child has the opportunity to increase his vocabulary considerably as he explores his surroundings and learns about new objects. Behaviour may at times be obstructive because of a desire to attempt self-feeding or do his own dressing, springing from an awareness of his independence and a desire to exercise this new capacity.

General History

How is he getting on?

Is he eating well, sleeping well and generally contented?

Is there anything which you would like to ask me about him?

Developmental History

(Short gestation must be allowed for, as before).

Motor

When did he begin to walk without help? (Usual age 13 months but with wide variations).

Language

Is he saying any words with meaning? How many? (Wide variation, but should be saying several words.)

Has he begun to make phrases or join words together, himself (not in imitation)? When did he begin? (Usual age 21-24 months — but some begin much sooner).

Everyday skills and social responses

Can he manage a cup — picking it up, drinking from it and putting it down, without much spilling? (Usual age 15 months). This depends very much on whether his mother lets him try to manage a cup. When was he first able to do this?

Can he feed himself with a spoon?

Does he copy you doing things about the house — brushing, sweeping, cleaning? (Domestic mimicry; begins 15-18 months).

When did he begin to tell you that he wants to use the pottie?

Does he tell you when he is about to urinate? (Average 18 to 24 months.) When did he begin to do so?

General Inspection

Watch the child as he walks round the clinic.

Watch him sitting or standing at a low table (Fig. 41) with appropriate toys in front of him. Note particularly mouthing, casting and drooling. Putting things to the mouth to explore them is at its peak from 6 to 10 months. By 12 to 15 months most children have grown out of this, and by 18 months it is definitely abnormal.

Fig. 41.

Casting, which consists of deliberately throwing one brick after another on to the floor, is a characteristic feature of the 12 to 15 month old baby; but he grows out of it, and its persistence after 18 months is abnormal.

Drooling (failing to control the saliva) has largely ceased by 15 months. It occasionally persists, however, even in normal children. Note whether the child is alert, responsive to people and objects around him and to his mother.

Gross Motor Performance

Observe whether he is walking and how well he walks, his stability and gait pattern (Fig. 42).

Lower Limbs. If he is not able to walk, examine as described for 10 months examination testing abduction of thighs, extension of legs and dorsiflexion of feet.

Vision and Fine Manipulation

See whether he looks at objects and reaches for and attains what he sees; note strabismus, nystagmus. While the child is playing at the table the examiner may gently hold his head while the child follows an object moved from side to side and up and down.

Notice how he shows interest in the human face, both close-to and at a distance of ten feet or more.

Give him several one inch cubes. He will probably be able to build a tower of two or three (Fig. 43). Notice how he uses *each* hand and whether there is any ataxia or tremor.

Hearing and Language

Observe the child's response to commands spoken quietly, out of sight.

Use sound-making toys if he does not respond to commands.

Listen to his speech. He is likely to vocalise freely, using tuneful jargon, and also to say some words clearly.

See whether he understands single requests — e.g. fetch a ball, give the teddy to mummy, where is your shoe?

Fig. 42.

Fig. 43.

47

Everyday Skills and Social Responses

See page 45 under Developmental History. Where possible, confirm mother's statements.

Significance of the Findings

If the examiner is uncertain of any finding, he will see the child again in one month. It would be wise to refer to a specialist for any of the following findings:

Any major anxiety in the mother.
Failure to stand or bear the weight on the legs.
Limited abduction of the hips.
Visual defect or squint.
Abnormality of the grasp.
Failure to respond to sound.
Failure to make spontaneous vocalisations.
Lack of interest and responsiveness: failure to look at the mother, failure to play meaningfully with toys.
Casting, mouthing and drooling — certainly if there are other signs of backwardness.

The Two-year-old Child

The two-year-old is an independent child who gets about, often rapidly, and is able to walk and run and negotiate stairs. Physical independence is matched by an increasing independence of spirit which requires to be maintained by periodically making contact with a familiar adult, usually a parent. Independence is also seen in attempts to do things for himself and to mimic some domestic activities. This is matched by the development of a well marked symbolisation enabling him to use language as a basis for concept formation, communication, and expression of his own ideas.

General History

How is he getting on?

Is he eating well, sleeping well and is he generally contented?

Is there anything which you would like to ask me about him?

Has he had any fits, ear trouble or other illnesses?

Developmental History

Motor

When did he begin to walk without help? (If not achieved at time of last visit).

Language

Does he join 2 or 3 words together into sentences? (Usual age of onset 21 to 24 months). One must be sure that the reply concerns spontaneously constructed speech and not merely imitation (e.g. of phrases like 'Oh dear').

If he is not talking, ask the mother 'Does he understand everything that you say to him?' and 'Will he do some things which you ask him to do?' (e.g. fetching his slippers, getting something out of the cupboard).

Will he come from another room if called? This provides a useful check on his hearing as well as on his understanding of spoken language. One must be sure that on being called, he comes without seeing his mother calling him.

Everyday skills and social responses

How does he play with his toys? The length of time he plays with any one toy is a guide to his powers of concentration. (One must distinguish, however, the obsessional play of a defective child with a single favourite toy). His manner of play indicates his understanding and his imagination (Fig. 44).

Does he feed himself without help? This includes, in particular, picking up a cup, drinking from it and putting it down without much spilling. The usual age for this is 15 months, but it depends greatly on the mother giving him a chance to feed himself instead of feeding him. Ask the mother whether she allows him to try to feed himself.

How much can he dress and undress himself? What can he get on and off unaided? This depends greatly on how much his mother allows him to try to dress himself, and, if, therefore, he is said to be unable to dress himself, one must ask his mother

49

Fig. 44.

how much she lets him try. (At 15 months many but not all children, if they have been given a chance, can, for instance, pull their pants up).

Is he clean and is he dry (a) by day, (b) by night? Children may say when they are about to urinate by the age of 18 months. Although some are dry at night by the age of 2 years, there is considerable variation in this and training need not be started till the age of 2 years. By 2 years old many children are dry by day and are dry by night at 3.

If he is said to be wet day and night, it is essential to ask whether there is constant dribbling of urine. One needs to know how long he can remain dry after passing urine (i.e. after having dry pants put on). If the mother insists that he is dribbling all the time, one should check the story by observing the mother putting dry pants on, and then seeing him in 15 minutes and again, if necessary, in 30 minutes, in order to determine whether he is still dry, and by watching the uncovered genitalia to see how frequently urine is passed.

True dribbling incontinence is a sign which urgently needs specialist investigation, in case there is a bladder neck or urethral obstruction or, in a girl, an ectopic ureter opening into the vagina or urethra.

General Inspection

Note his interest in his surroundings, his concentration on a toy, his responsiveness. Look for strabismus or nystagmus.

Observe casting, mouthing or dribbling. At 2 years old any of these is likely to be abnormal.

Gross Motor Performance

Note how he walks (Fig. 45), particularly the length of stride, steadiness and ease with which he moves from sitting or standing to walking. Inability to walk and marked asymmetry of gait are likely to be abnormal.

50

Vision and Fine Manipulation

His vision is tested by showing him small toys, held 10 feet away from him, and asking him to match them with corresponding toys on the tray in front of him or to name them (See also Figs. 53 and 54, page 56.)

Hearing and Language

One makes simple commands in a soft voice. One asks him to identify parts of the body (where is your nose, mouth, eyes, foot? etc.). At 2 years the average child can identify at least 4 parts.

Listen for the quality and quantity of speech and see whether there is sentence formation. It is helpful to write down the sounds of what he says at the time and then to interpret this later.

At 2 years old most children are making short phrases and are usually intelligible.

Fig. 45. This two-year-old is walking competently, while carrying a box of bricks and a rather large book.

Fig. 46. The child has been asked to comb her hair and in doing so, shows good coordination.

Everyday Skills and Social Responses

While the examiner is talking to the mother, the child should have access to toys, miniature cars, cups and saucers, furniture, spread out on a low table. The examiner can see whether he uses the toys meaningfully and observes his manipulative skill (Fig. 46). The 2 year old child can usually build a tower of 6 to 7 cubes. As he builds, note ataxia, tremor or clumsiness.

Put five or six cubes in a line and add one cube to the first (as a chimney to the train), and then ask him to do the same. At 2 years he is likely to align two or more cubes, but will not add a chimney.

Given a pencil and paper, he may imitate a vertical stroke made by the examiner. He is shown a book, and asked to identify two or three objects ('Show me the house, show me the pussy'). The examiner observes him turning the pages. The average child of 18 months turns two or three pages at a time; at 2 years he turns pages singly.

Significance of Findings

If the examiner is uncertain or finds minor degrees of abnormality, he will re-examine in one to three months. The following findings indicate the need of referral to a specialist:—

Any major anxiety in the mother.

Failure to walk.

Tremor or ataxia on building bricks.

Casting, mouthing, drooling.

Visual defect, strabismus, nystagmus, cataract.

Absence of speech, or speech confined to a few single words.

Defective interest and concentration.

Any other retardation in development.

Fig. 47. The child was asked to give Mummy a cup of tea, the examiner being careful to say this quietly behind the child and not to point at the tea-set on the table, which the child was already inspecting. She has poured out the imaginary cup of tea and given it to her mother.

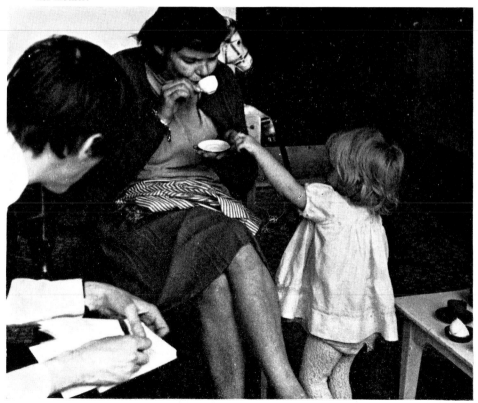

The Three-year-old Child

The 3-year-old has had more than a year to practise a large variety of physical skills and is quicker to move, more sure footed, and is enthusiastic about playing at jumping, climbing and attempting to throw and catch a ball despite the fact that performance is still rudimentary. His physical independence and confidence is usually matched by an increasing sense of security and tolerance of being left for short periods, but this security is still very tenuous and the support of familiar surroundings and 'minder' is needed. Furthermore the explorations into 'fantasy land' which are reflected in the increasing imaginativeness of his play and his love of playing parts makes him very susceptible to frightening situations. Speech is well established and is used to communicate demands and ideas, to tell a story of truth or fantasy and to direct his play activity.

General History

How is he getting on?

Is he eating well, sleeping well and is he generally contented?

Is there anything which you would like to ask about him?

Had he had any fits, ear trouble or other illnesses?

Developmental History

Everyday skills and social responses

Can he use a cup and can he use a spoon to feed himself without help?

Is he dressing himself, apart from buttons and shoe laces? (Usual age 3 years). This varies considerably depending greatly on whether the mother has given him a chance to be independent.

Does he say 'No' or refuse to do things when asked? (This 'negativism' is, of course, a step forward, and not naughtiness).

How does he play meaningfully with his toys? How long will he play with any one toy? (Distinguish obsessional play, as before).

Is he dry and clean in the day and the night? As before, if he is said to be constantly wet, the examiner will himself make sure about dribbling.

When in doubt about his development in one field only, such as speech, ask how he compares with his siblings in the other fields and in this one. (Check that the siblings are apparently normal).

Inquire about his social environment. Does his mother play with him? Have they a garden? Does he meet other children, does he go to a nursery or nursery school?

General Inspection

As with the two-year-old, one observes his general behaviour and remarks specifically any more infantile behaviour. Strabismus and nystagmus may have developed since the previous examination.

Fig. 49. The three-year-old indulges in complicated imaginative play. The pigs have been put into the pig-sty and the cow is in the field. The child is loading the milk-cans into the cart to go to market.

Fig. 48.

Gross Motor Performance

Note the child's gait as he runs around.

Ask him to stand first on one foot, then on the other, without holding on (average age 3 years) (Fig. 48).

Vision and Fine Manipulation

Watch the child's handling of small objects (Fig. 49).

Give him 10 one inch cubes. Ask him to build a tower (tower of 9 cubes, usually at 3 years). He will also make a 'train' from the blocks if the examiner shows him what is wanted (Figs. 50 and 51).

Ask him to imitate the construction of a bridge with three cubes, i.e. make the bridge, leave it in front of him, and ask him to do the same. (Usual age for this 3 years).

Ask him to imitate horizontal and vertical strokes with pencil and paper. (Usual age 2 years) (Fig. 52).

Draw a circle out of his sight and ask him to copy it (usual age for copying a circle, 3 years). If he fails to copy a circle, you can ask him to *imitate* a circle. Ask him to watch you as you draw a circle, and then ask him to do the same. This is achieved at a younger age than 3 years.

Test near vision and also at 10 feet away, using Sheridan's STYCAR 5 letter matching and other tests. If possible, test vision of each eye separately.

See whether he can match the colours of cubes of different colours; matching colours is usually done at 3 years.

Ask what colour the cube is. Basic colours are usually named at 3 years.

Hearing and Language

See whether the child will obey simple instructions spoken from a distance of 10 feet, but don't let him see your lip movements. (Hold a card in front of your mouth).

Ask him to point to his nose, eyes, mouth (usual before 3 years).

Ask him the name of a knife, penny, key (usual at age 3 years).

By the age of $2\frac{1}{2}$ most children refer to themselves as 'I' or 'me'.

Everyday Skills and Social Responses

Observe his interest and concentration. Look particularly for aimless over-activity.

Observe his responsiveness to his mother.

Note any drooling or mouthing.

Ask him his name and sex (usual age for knowing this, 3 years).

Ask him to *repeat digits* ('Say after me, 682') Try three different digits, three times. (Usual age for repeating 2 digits in one out of three trials is $2\frac{1}{2}$ years; 3 digits in one of three trials 3 years).

Fig. 50.   **Fig. 51** (*top*) **and Fig. 52** (*lower*).

Significance of Findings

If an abnormality is doubtful or slight, the child is seen again in one to three months to re-assess. The following findings indicate the need to refer him to a specialist:—

Any major anxiety in the mother.

Dribbling incontinence.

Ataxia, tremor, unsteady or abnormal gait.

Poor visual response, strabismus.

Doubt about hearing, failure to talk in sentences, indistinct speech. Children with any of these should have the hearing tested by a specialist *and* have the nature of the indistinctness evaluated by a competent person, *and* see a paediatrician for comprehensive assessment.

Aimless overactivity.

Any other retardation in development.

Evidence suggesting emotional deprivation, lack of stimulation or seriously poor social situation.

Figs. 53 and 54. At three, the child is asked to carry out a 5-letter matching test from the Sheridan-Stycar eye-testing equipment. If she fails to perform this, she is asked to match the small toys from the STYCAR set. The examiner should be 10ft. away.

The Four-and-a-half-year-old Child

It is our belief that children should have a full and comprehensive examination just before or soon after they start school. The age at which school starts varies in different countries. It is 5 years old in the United Kingdom and 6 in the United States, for example. Although it is currently our aim to see that all children are regularly screened during the early years of life, it will be some decades, even in developed countries, before this is achieved, and where the child has not been assessed by a doctor for two or three years it is wise to carry out a thorough examination when the child approaches school. When he arrives at school new demands are made upon him and skills which he has not yet been required to use are expected of him. Furthermore, in the intervening years since he was first seen illness may have occurred which may have had sequelae which were not identified at the time of the illness. Whatever the reasons, there is some evidence that at least 5 per cent of children in ordinary school suffer from what have been called neurodevelopmental disorders of childhood. These include minor visual, auditory and motor disabilities and visuomotor and language deficits which can lead to major interference with education. Every effort should be made to detect these children. We believe that by their early recognition a great deal of help can be given to the children and that their identification will greatly help the teacher in her difficult task of handling large numbers of young children.

The timing of this examination is difficult. In the United Kingdom at the moment there is a statutory duty for an examination at the age of 5. It has been suggested by the Plowden Committee (1967) that it is desirable for this examination to take place prior to the child's entry into school, but there are at present considerable practical difficulties about this administratively and there are also some advantages to the doctor seeing the child when he has been in the school for a little time and settled down. This enables the doctor to have closer consultation with the teachers who are supervising the child's work. In this volume we have not concerned ourselves with this important examination and our examination at $4\frac{1}{2}$ years is the final of the pre-school routine screening tests. If, however, it should become the 'pre-school examination' it should be expanded.

The four and a half year old is sturdy and able to walk fairly long distances, to run, to climb with considerable agility, to skip, and probably to hop. Many will have had their first experience of riding a small tricycle. The child is now able to play alongside and in cooperation with others at home or at a nursery school. Such play increases his opportunities for make-believe play in which he may, in the role of a child or an adult, act out his understanding of the outside world and of others. Conversation with a four year old can be a great delight. Speech is usually clear and ideas of considerable depth are often expressed in fairly long sentences. Understanding of the processes of sharing and taking turns is now beginning to develop. This increasing maturity, both social and emotional, is important for the child on the threshold of school entry.

The General History

How is he getting on?

Is there anything which you would like to ask me about?

Does he eat well, sleep well and is he a generally contented child?

Has he had any fits, ear discharge (other than wax) or other illnesses?

Developmental History

Can he hop and skip (often but not always by 4 years)?

Is he learning to be on his own? Does he get on with other children?

Can he now dress himself fully? He may be dressed by his mother because she likes to do this, partly because it is quicker.

Inquire about social situation, opportunities for play with other children.

General Inspection

Note general appearance in terms of alertness, interest, concentration and how he does things.

Note clumsiness, ataxia or tremor.

Gross Motor Performance

Ask him to stand first on one foot and then on the other.

Ask him to hop; only about half will do it alone, but most children will make a good attempt if one hand is held. Girls seem to learn this skill earlier than boys. Both sexes usually learn to hop on the non-dominant foot first.

Vision and Fine Manipulation

Look for strabismus. Test near vision and at ten feet with both eyes and with each eye occluded in turn (Sheridan STYCAR 7 letter matching test). Children do not complain of poor vision. Vision *must* be tested.

Give him 10 one inch cubes: Construct a gate and ask him to copy it. (Usually at 4 years). Ask him to construct a bridge from a model. (Usually at $3\frac{1}{2}$ years). See Fig. 55 a and b. Note any clumsiness, tremor or ataxia.

Give him pencil and paper and ask him to copy a cross, circle and a square (drawn out of his sight). A circle is copied at $3\frac{1}{2}$, a cross at 4 and a square at 5 years by most normal children. Observe the way he holds a pencil; at $4\frac{1}{2}$ years this is usually a mature grasp between thumb, forefinger and middle finger.

A simple test of the child's comprehension is his ability to repeat 3 or 4 digits after the examiner.

Hearing and Language

Test hearing, using pictures, toys or spoken instructions.

Hearing *must* be tested, as it is not always possible to provoke much spontaneous speech and in this connection the mother's story is not always reliable. Do STYCAR test for hearing high frequencies (picture and 'ph', 'th' tests at 10 feet. (Fig. 56).

Note his speech, including sentence formation and any substitution of consonants or stuttering.

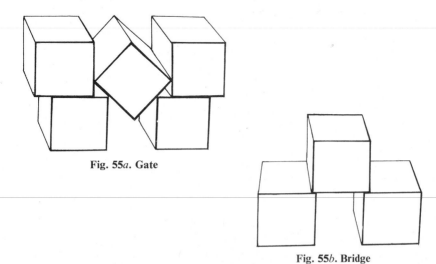

Fig. 55*a*. Gate

Fig. 55*b*. Bridge

Fig. 56.

Everyday Skills and Social Responses

Note how he meets and relates to other people. Unless he is in a shy phase, most children at this age should, by the end of the examination, be able to have a conversation with the examiner. The easiest topic is his own home and he should be able to tell one something of the activities of members of his immediate family.

Significance of Findings

The following are indications for referral to a specialist:

Any major anxiety in the mother.

Clumsiness or any delay in motor development.

Suspected or possible defect of vision.

Poor intelligibility of speech (to people outside the family), substitutions, stuttering.

Language delay.

Poor concentration, distractability, aimless overactivity.

Behaviour difficulties.

Any notable backwardness in performance.

Evidence suggesting serious social deprivation.

Interpretation

All Babies are Different

In arriving at a developmental assessment, the doctor always remembers that babies vary tremendously in the various aspects of their development. He is therefore cautious in diagnosing abnormality, for the child may be a normal child who is slow to mature. But it is not right to use this as an excuse for not making every attempt to detect developmental delay or for not referring a child for another opinion.

A truly average baby, who is average in all aspects of development, is rare. Babies differ not only because their potential and eventual levels of intellectual capacity inevitably cover a wide span, but because, as a result of their inheritance and environment, there are familial and individual patterns of development in each field. In some families there is a pronounced tendency to early motor development, with consequent early sitting and walking, whereas in another family several members may show a pronounced delay in motor development without any motor or intellectual handicap. These variations have little or nothing to do with the child's intelligence. When the child is backward in one or two fields of development, one suspects a handicap in this field or these fields. *A mentally-handicapped child is backward in all fields of development, except occasionally in sitting and walking, and occasionally in sphincter control.*

An intellectually handicapped child without cerebral palsy is likely to be relatively less retarded in the sitting and walking aspects of development. (The child with cerebral palsy is likely to be more retarded in sitting and walking than in other fields.) The backward child will be late in showing good visual and auditory responses, in his understanding of symbols and spoken language and, later, in the development of speech; he will show some lack of general alertness, interest in the surroundings and concentration and he will be late in acquiring simple everyday skills.

Under the age of five years, accurate forecasting of intelligence is not possible, although extreme intellectual handicap can be identified. Even if a child seems to be backward in all fields and hence probably intellectually handicapped, it is still wise to be extremely cautious in what is said to the mother and to others. The child may be described as 'generally retarded'. It is better not to label him with any numerical quotient, even a developmental quotient, as false conclusions as to the future I.Q. are too often drawn from such numerical quotients.

Some babies are temporarily slow in their development

A few babies who show delay in almost all aspects of development, later prove to be normal. This may be a familial feature, but it occurs sometimes without such a history. It may be difficult to distinguish such a baby from a mentally handicapped one. The following features would make one think that the child may well prove to be mentally normal:—

(1) Family history of the same feature.
(2) Good degree of alertness, interest, responsiveness.
(3) Head of normal size in relation to his weight.

It is essential to follow up such babies, and to keep an accurate record of their progress.

Abnormal signs may go

Even when, in early developmental screenings, there is developmental delay associated with abnormal neurological signs, the signs may completely disappear and the delay resolve. Even asymmetry of muscle tone, suggesting a spastic hemiplegia, may disappear completely. Such children should however be carefully followed up, as they may display specific learning difficulties when they reach school or turn out to be 'clumsy' children.

Causes of variations in developmental progress

Wide variations occur in children who are mentally and physically normal, but if a child is definitely delayed in one field of development, it is essential to exclude or establish the presence of any underlying handicap or handicaps, so that, if necessary, treatment can be given. Any child with delay must be referred to a paediatrician for further assessment and evaluation. On the other hand if a child's performance falls outside the range described, it must not be firmly concluded, let alone announced as certain, that he is necessarily abnormal but only that he is at present late in his development and needs further study. One has occasionally seen a child who was unable to sit unsupported until 12 months, or to walk unsupported until 24 months or later, who later proved to be normal. Such delay in locomotion will delay his learning about the world and may worry the parents. *The further he is from the average in a particular skill, the more likely it is that he is abnormal and in need of detailed assessment and perhaps treatment.* It is certainly wise to refer to an expert any child who shows definite delay in acquisition of any of the various skills, and imperative if the delay is considerable.

In any discussion with the mother, it is wise to avoid using the word 'backward'; one can speak of his being late in acquiring a skill. Similarly it is wise not to say 'a child *should* be walking by 18 months'; say 'children *usually* walk by 18 months'.

What to say to the mother

Because abnormal neurological signs may disappear and because a normal child may exhibit delayed development, *it is wise to observe extreme caution before telling a mother that her child is a spastic or is backward.* If there is doubt it is usually possible to say nothing until the examination has been repeated. But some mothers will perceive the doctor's uncertainty and if nothing is said they may conclude that the situation is more serious than it is. It is usually best for the doctor to be open, admitting his doubts. If he is referring the child to an expert, he may tell the mother he is not certain but that he expects she too would like a second opinion; that if necessary the child will be able to have early treatment and that it is possible that it may turn out that there is nothing wrong.

If cerebral palsy is so mild that one cannot be sure, no harm will be done by waiting. On the other hand, if there is doubt about a child's hips, if a child over the age of six months has any strabismus even if intermittent or if there is any doubt about the baby's hearing, expert attention must be sought without delay.

Developmental assessment is a skill of great difficulty. It is most dangerous for a doctor to think it is easy. We have repeatedly seen the gravest anxiety occasioned by doctors who jumped to their own conclusions without seeking early expert advice. Mothers have been told that their child was 'possibly spastic' or 'possibly backward' when the mother herself did not suspect any abnormality. If she does suspect an abnormality and asks whether the child is normal, the doctor must express his opinion, but if he is not an expert he should seek specialist advice.

RECOMMENDED FURTHER READING

BAYLEY, NANCY (1961) *Revised manual of directions for an infant scale of menta motor development:* New York: Psychological Corporation.

GESELL, ARNOLD (5th Edn., 1966) *The First Five Years of Life:* London: Methuen.

GRIFFITHS, RUTH (1954) *The Abilities of Babies:* London: University of London Press.

ILLINGWORTH, R. S. (3rd Edn., 1966) *The Development of the Infant and the Young Child, Normal and Abnormal:* E. & S. Livingstone, Edinburgh and London.

ILLINGWORTH, R. S. (1961, reprinted 1966) *An Introduction to Developmental Assessment in the First Year:* London: Little Club Clinics in Developmental Medicine/William Heinemann Medical Books Ltd.

PEIPER, A. (1963) *Cerebral Function in Infancy and Childhood:* New York: Consultants Bureau Enterprises Inc.,: London: Pitman Medical Publishing Co. Ltd.

PRECHTL, HEINZ and BEINTEMA, DAVID (1964, reprinted 1965) *Neurological Examination of the Full Term Newborn Infant:* London: Little Club Clinics in Developmental Medicine/William Heinemann Medical Books Ltd.

SHERIDAN, MARY D. (2nd Edn., 1968) *The Developmental Progress of Infants and Young Children:* London: H.M.S.O.

THE 'STYCAR' VISION & HEARING TESTS

These tests, which Dr. Sheridan prepared, are distributed by The National Foundation for Educational Research in England and Wales, The Mere, Upton Park, Slough, Bucks.

The vision tests are designed to give reliable information of the distant and near vision of normal children between 2 and 7 years, and of handicapped children of a corresponding mental ability. The tests include miniature toys which the child is required to match at a distance and letter tests with key cards and charts and a manual which describes their use with young children.

The hearing tests include sound-making toys, picture vocabulary cards and a full manual giving details of how the tests should be administered.

Acknowledgements

We are grateful to the following for their kind permission to reproduce various figures:
Dr. Gerhard Nellhaus; the American Academy of Paediatrics and the publishers of 'Paediatrics' (Head circumference charts, pages 3 and 4).
Professor J. M. Tanner and J. & A. Churchill Ltd. (Head circumference tables, pages 3 and 4).
Professor Heinz Prechtl and Dr. D. J. Beintema (Figs. 6, 7, 8, 13a, b).
Professor A. Milani-Comparetti and Dr. E. Anna Gidoni (Figs. 14 a, b, c, 15 and 16).
Dr. Richmond S. Paine, Dr. Thomas E. Oppe and the W. B. Saunders Co., Philadelphia (Figs. 16a and 19).
E. & S. Livingstone Ltd. (Figs. 12, 24, 34, 35 and 38); previously published in R. S. Illingworth's 'The Development of the Infant and Young Child'.

REFERENCES

Mac Keith, R. C. (1964) 'The primary walking response and its facilitation by passive extension of the head.' *Acta paediat. lat.*, **17**, Suppl. No. 6.
Milani-Comparetti, A., Gidoni, E. A. (1967) 'Routine developmental examination in normal and retarded children.' *Develop. Med. Child Neurol.*, **9**, 631.
Paine, Richmond S. (1964) 'The evolution of infantile postural reflexes in the presence of chronic brain syndromes.' *Develop. Med. Child Neurol*, **6**, 345.
Plowden Committee (1967) 'Children and their Primary Schools'; A Report of the Central Advisory Council for Education (England). London: H.M.S.O.
Sheridan, M. D. (1958) 'Simple clinical hearing tests for very young or mentally retarded children.' *Brit. med. J.*, **2**, 999.
—— (1960) 'Vision screening of very young or handicapped children.' *Brit. med. J.*, **2**, 453.
—— (1964) 'Disorders of communication in young children.' *Monthly Bull. Min. Health*, **23**. 20.
—— (1969) 'Vision screening procedures for very young or handicapped children' *in* Aspects of Developmental & Paediatric Ophthalmology. London: Spastics International Medical Publications/William Heinemann Medical Books Ltd.